CHILDREN'S REFERENCE
LIVING PLANET

Capella

This edition published in 2008 by Arcturus Publishing Limited
26/27 Bickels Yard, 151–153 Bermondsey Street,
London SE1 3HA

Copyright © 2008 Arcturus Publishing Limited

ISBN: 978-1-84193-820-2

Designers: Q2A India and Talking Design
Editors: Rebecca Gerlings and Alex Woolf

Printed in China

Contents

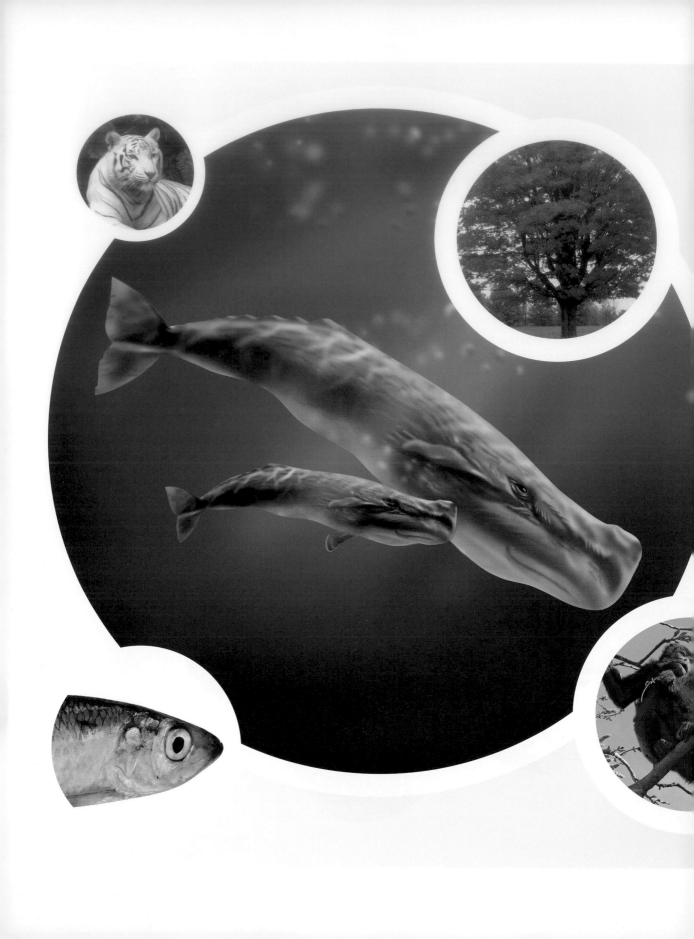

Introduction

Life is everywhere on Earth. Organisms survive and thrive in every environment, from the frozen tundra of the North Pole to the steaming rainforests near the equator; from the permanent night of the ocean floor to several miles up in the air. Life has even been found in extreme places such as around superhot undersea thermal vents or in groundwater thousands of feet below the Earth's surface. In the 3.7 billion years that life has existed on this planet, organisms have diversified and adapted to almost every condition imaginable.

In this book, you will discover many fascinating facts about life on Earth. Do you know, for example, which monkey uses different alarm calls depending on the type of predator? Or which big cat can climb a tree while carrying an antelope three times its size? Which bird flies 18,640 miles (30,000 km) between the Arctic and Antarctic each year? And which mammal can dive beneath the sea to a depth of 2,300 feet (700 m) and stay there for over an hour? You can find out the answers to these questions and many more in the pages of this book.

Mammals

Mammals are vertebrates (animals with a backbone) that suckle their young. They are warm-blooded animals with highly developed organs and four limbs. Most mammals are covered with hair or fur and almost all have teeth that can cut and chew food. Mammals can be found in all kinds of habitats, including the hottest and the coldest regions of the planet. Some common animals, including elephants, lions, whales, dolphins, cats, dogs, and even humans, are mammals.

Key facts:

• The blue whale is not only the largest mammal, but it is also the largest living animal in the world. It can grow to a length of more than 98 feet (30 meters). The smallest of all mammals in the world is the Kitti's hog-nosed bat. This tiny bat is as small as a bumblebee.

• Most mammals have a long life span. Horses and dogs can live up to 20 years; chimpanzees have been known to live longer than 50 years. However, humans live the longest, with an average life span of 80 years. Some people live to the ripe old age of 110 or sometimes even longer.

• Each year, grey whales migrate between the Arctic waters and the Mexican coast, covering a total distance of 12,427 miles (20,000 kilometers). This is the largest distance covered by any migrating animal on the planet. Only the Arctic tern, a bird, covers a distance longer than that. The Arctic tern flies over 22,000 miles (35,405 kilometers) to reach its new home.

There are over 5,000 species of mammals in the world. They have been divided into various families, including primates, big cats, hoofed animals, rodents, and canines. The rodent family consists of about 2,000 species, including rats, squirrels, beavers, moles, and mice. All meat-eating mammals belong to the group, carnivore, while plant-eating mammals make up the group, herbivore. Carnivores include big cats like lions and tigers, bears, wolves, foxes, and marine mammals such as seals and walruses. Herbivores include deer, horses, rhinoceros, antelope, camels, giraffes, hippopotamuses, and zebras. All mammals with hooves are called ungulates and are further divided into even-toed and odd-toed ungulates. We belong to a family called primates. This family includes monkeys, apes, and lemurs. Some mammals spend their whole life or part of their life in water. Such mammals, including whales, seals, dolphins, sea lions, walruses, and manatees, form the family of marine mammals.

Smart mammals

Mammals are the most intelligent of all animals. They are able to think, learn fast, and imitate actions. The brain of a mammal, like that of other vertebrates, is divided into three parts—hindbrain, midbrain, and forebrain. The hindbrain controls bodily functions like breathing. The midbrain deals with nerve impulses and the forebrain helps a mammal to think and respond to its surroundings. The forebrain is highly developed with millions of nerve cells. Among mammals, humans are considered to be the most intelligent.

▲ **Mum's the word**
Most mammals give birth to live young and look after their babies until they can take care of themselves.

▶ **Footsie**
The feet of each mammal are adapted to that mammal's habitat and position in the food chain.

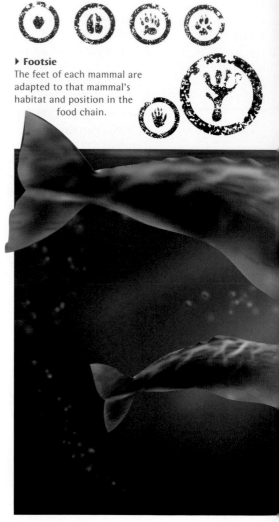

Defense tactics

Most mammals depend on their excellent senses and reflexes to escape from dangerous situations. Smaller mammals usually flee. Mammals like skunks release foul-smelling chemicals to deter the enemy, while porcupines have spines that are erected in times of danger. Larger mammals use their limbs and teeth to cause serious injury to their attacker.

Mammalian diet

Mammals eat food not only to grow, but also to keep themselves warm. That is why they eat more often than cold-blooded animals like reptiles, fish, and amphibians. The smaller the mammal, the bigger its appetite. This is because small mammals lose heat faster than larger mammals. The teeth of mammals are highly specialized and adapted to their individual diet, but all mammals have teeth that fit together when the mouth is closed. This allows them to carry out a variety of processes like gnawing, biting, and chewing.

Smaller mammals feed on insects and worms, while bigger meat-eating mammals hunt down other mammals and birds. The senses of smell, sight, and hearing are highly developed in all mammals, but in mammals that hunt these senses are heightened. Herbivorous mammals have a stomach that helps them to digest the plants they eat. Almost all herbivores spend a long time chewing their food since certain plant parts are difficult to digest.

Try these too:

Primates (p 10–11), Big cats (p 12–13), Marine Mammals (p 20–23), Birds (p 16–17), Reptiles (p 20–21), Amphibians (p 22–23)

▾ **Tooth matters**
Carnivores have specialized teeth that help them to crush bones and tear through flesh.

How they move

Most small mammals, such as rodents, have four limbs that are almost equal. They run and climb using all four of their limbs. Primates are good climbers. Some can also hang from branches of trees. Most heavy mammals keep their feet flat on the ground while walking. This does not allow for fast movement. So, hunting mammals walk on the pads of their toes with their heels off the ground enabling them to run fast. Hoofed animals have hard hooves and long strides that help them to run quickly, and for long periods of time. Mammals like kangaroos hop on their hind legs. Some mammals, such as flying squirrels, have flaps of skin that act like wings to help them to glide from tree to tree.

▲ **To greener pastures!**
Many large mammals are known to migrate. Animal migration is influenced by climate and food supply. Whales migrate to warmer waters during the breeding season. Animals, such as zebras, migrate in search of water. Herbivores that live in the Arctic regions migrate to warmer climates during the winter.

◀ **Flipper power**
Marine mammals have flippers instead of legs to help them swim better.

Primates

Monkeys, apes (gorillas, chimpanzees, gibbons, and orang-utans), and humans make up the order called *primate*. All primates have five flexible fingers and toes, opposable thumbs, arms and legs that move more freely than other mammals, forward-facing eyes enabling them to judge distances accurately, and large brains.

▶ **Aping about**
Apes are found only in Asia and Africa. They have arms that are longer than their legs and do not have tails.

Key facts:

• The gorilla is the largest primate in the world. The adult male can be as tall as a full-grown man and can weigh a maximum of 375 pounds (170 kilograms).

• The world's smallest primate is the pygmy mouse lemur found in Madagascar. This animal is only 8 inches (20 centimeters) tall and weighs about 1 ounce (30 grams).

• African vervet monkeys use different alarm calls for each of their main predators—eagles, leopards, and snakes. The monkeys react differently to each call. When they hear the eagle alarm call, the monkeys hide among dense vegetation. At the sound of the leopard call they climb as high as possible. They simply go "on alert" at the snake call.

▶ **Strong shoulders**
Primates have a collarbone that helps to stabilize the shoulder. This is vital for a primate since the shoulders support its body weight while hanging down from branches with its arms.

Primates are commonly found in tropical jungles, dry forests, grasslands, and cold, mountainous regions. There are more than 350 species of primates in the world. They are broadly divided into prosimians and anthropoids. The prosimians, or "primitive primates," consist of only 60 species, including lemurs and lorises. The rest fall under the anthropoid category. The term *anthropoid* means "humanlike." This group consists of about 175 species. Most anthropoids have flat faces and a poor sense of smell. They depend on their eyesight to find food. Opposable thumbs and big toes help primates to grip branches as well as pick up objects. Most monkeys and prosimians have tails, which help them to maintain balance while moving from tree to tree. Many species have prehensile tails that can be wrapped around branches and act like an extra foot or hand.

Monkeys from Asia and Africa are known as Old World monkeys. Like humans and apes, these monkeys have narrow noses and downward-facing nostrils. These monkeys are also called catarrhines, meaning downward-nosed. Monkeys from Central and South America have broad noses and nostrils that open sideways. These monkeys are called platyrrhines, meaning broad-nosed. Platyrrhines are more commonly known as New World monkeys.

Primate diet

Most primates are omnivorous, meaning they eat both meat and plants. However, there are a few species that live entirely on either meat or plants. Most monkeys are opportunistic feeders, meaning they will eat whatever they come across, including bird eggs, fruit, and plant sap. Several species of monkeys even attack and eat other monkeys. Some monkeys love to eat leaves. Howler monkeys of South America and colobus monkeys of Africa eat the leaves of any tree. The digestive system of leaf-eating monkeys is similar to that of other herbivores like deer and cows.

Fussy monkey

The proboscis monkey, which is found on the island of Borneo, is very selective about its food. It usually prefers to eat the leaves of mangrove and pedada trees, although it feeds on seeds and green fruit when its favorite is unavailable.

Primate language

Primates use several methods of communication. Solitary species use scent as a means of communication. Urine, feces, or special scent glands are used to mark territory or to announce a particular individual's desire to mate. Primates that live in groups use both visual and vocal signals. The majority of monkeys and apes communicate visually using a variety of facial expressions, some of which are very similar to those we humans use. Sound is yet another important mode of communication. Primates use a wide array of sounds, from soft clicks and grunts to elaborate songs and roars. Courtship calls are loud and vary with each species. Chimpanzees have been known to use as many as 34 different vocal signals. One of these calls is used to communicate the location of food.

Behavior

Primates, especially anthropoid primates, are the most intelligent of all animals. They are extremely curious and are quick to learn. They usually learn by imitating. Primates are completely dependant on their power of sight to move about and to locate food. Species that live in groups are highly interactive. They clean and groom each other's fur. Their high level of intelligence has enabled primates to learn several new skills, including making tools. This skill is most pronounced in humans, followed by chimpanzees.

▼ **Healthy relationships**
Removing parasites from the fur of other members of the group helps many primates to forge new relationships and maintain old ones.

◀ **Tarsier terror**
Tarsiers have long back legs that are used to leap onto their prey. They then hold the prey down with their hands and kill it with sharp, pointed teeth.

Try these too:

Mammals (p 8–9),
Big Cats (p 12–13),
Reptiles (p 20–21),
Amphibians (p 22–23),
Insects (p 24–25),
Plant Life (p 26–27)

▼ **Howl to be heard**
The barking sound made by howler monkeys can be heard 1.9 miles (3 kilometers) away. It is this sound that gives the monkey its name.

Big Cats

From the graceful domestic cat to the more ferocious species, cats are truly amazing animals. All cats are carnivorous and hunt smaller animals. They usually hunt at night, but tigers prefer to hunt at dawn or dusk. Cats have large eyes, sharp teeth, a good sense of hearing, and powerful limbs with sharp claws. Most of them have long tails and coats that have patterns. Lions, tigers, leopards, and jaguars all belong to the group called big cats.

▲ **Multi-purpose tongue**
A cat's tongue has hooklike projections called papillae. Cats use their tongue to clean the flesh from the bones of their prey and to groom themselves.

Key facts:

• The jaguar uses its powerful jaws and sharp teeth to pierce the skull of its prey between the ears. The jaguar's strong teeth can even break open turtle shells.

• White tigers are not a result of albinism. A true albino would not have stripes, but white tigers have very prominent stripes. The color variation is due to mutation. White tigers rarely occur naturally. They are usually bred in captivity and so can only be seen in zoos.

• Lionesses do most of the hunting, while lions mainly defend the pride. The large golden mane of the lion gives it away while hunting.

All cats have small faces and short, broad skulls. They have strong jaws with three pairs of incisor teeth, one pair of canines, two or three pairs of premolars, and one pair of molars. Cat paws have soft pads. The forelimbs have five toes and the hind limbs have four. All cats walk on their toes with the heel raised off the ground. They also have long, sharp claws that can be drawn into their paw. The cheetah is the only cat that cannot retract its claws. All cats are sticklers for cleanliness and spend a lot of time licking their body, and cleaning and rubbing their face with their paws.

Feline senses

Big cats are specialist hunters that rely on their senses of sight and hearing to locate their prey. The eyes of the cat face forward, which helps them to judge distances and the size of their prey accurately. Their large pupils allow more light to enter their eyes at night.

▶ **Show of strength**
Leopards are extremely strong animals. They have been known to carry full-grown antelopes, which are about three times their size, up to treetops to eat in peace.

During the day, the pupils can be shrunk into slits, allowing less light to enter the eyes. Cat ears can be round or pointed. They are held erect and can be turned in any direction to pick up the slightest sounds. Cats also have long whiskers that help them to feel their way around. The whiskers are very sensitive to movement and touch. Sometimes, cats use their whiskers to locate hidden prey.

◀ **Burning bright!**
Some big cats' pupils appear circular when dilated and, as in domestic cats, mirrorlike tissue in their retinas reflects the light back, making their eyes glow in the dark.

Coat of many patterns

Big cats have fur coats that protect them from extreme heat and cold. The tiger has a striped coat that allows the cat to conceal itself in vegetation while hunting. Lions have sand-colored coats that help them to blend into the landscape of the open savannahs. Leopards and jaguars have spots that serve as good camouflage. The spots of jaguars are more like paw prints and are different from those of leopards. Like the fingerprints of humans, leopard and jaguar spots are unique—no two individuals have the same spots.

Hunting tactics

Most big cats are too large to run fast, therefore they usually use a combination of speed and stealth to hunt. Lions prefer to creep up on their unsuspecting prey. If the prey bolts, the lion chases it.

If the prey is too fast the lion gives up the chase. Tigers like to stalk their prey. They hide in the tall grass, waiting for the prey to pass by. Then they pounce on it. Tigers can leap up to 30 feet (9 meters), making it one of the most successful hunters. The leopard also uses stealth tactics to capture prey, which it then carries off to the top of a tree so that no other animals can steal its food.

Behavior

Lions are social animals. They live in groups called "prides." A typical pride consists of 3 to 30 individuals, but on average have 4 to 6. One to five adult lions and several lionesses and cubs make up a pride. Tigers, jaguars, and leopards, on the other hand, are solitary creatures. They come together only during the mating season. All big cats are territorial. Tigers leave claw marks on the bark of trees and a urine trail to let other tigers know that the territory is occupied. Jaguars and leopards also mark their territories in a similar fashion. Both tigers and jaguars are good swimmers and can often be seen lazing in ponds and lakes.

◀ **Judge by the cover**
The coat of each big cat contains a unique pattern that serves as a camouflage and helps in the identification of the particular species.

▲ **On guard**
Adult lions and lionesses are fierce when it comes to protecting their pride.

Try these too:

Birds (p 16–17),
Fish (p 18–19),
Reptiles (p 20–21),
Amphibians (p 22–23)

Color variations

Melanism—the over-production of a skin pigment, melanin—is common among jaguars and leopards. Affected animals are black in color and are commonly referred to as black panthers, but are not a separate species as, on closer examination, the typical spots of a jaguar or a leopard can be seen. Albinism—the absence of pigment—is rare among cats, but has been reported in some jaguars and leopards. These individuals are called white panthers. White tigers, however, are not albinos, nor are they a separate subspecies, but are the result of a recessive gene.

Marine Mammals

Some mammals spend most of their life, or at least part of it, in oceans. These marine mammals have special features that help them to adapt to their surroundings. These animals share many characteristics with other mammals, but are different in some ways. Unlike most other mammals, marine mammals do not have hair.

Key facts:

- Whales use a series of moans and clicks to communicate between themselves. Most of these sounds are either too low or too high for humans to be able to hear. Blue whales and fin whales produce the loudest noises of all animals.

- Weddell seals are the best divers of all seals. They can dive to depths of 2,300 feet (700 meters) and stay there for over an hour.

- Toothed whales give out sound waves that bounce off an object, helping them to identify the size, shape and location of that object. Most toothed whales use this method, called echolocation, to locate prey, enemies or other members of their pod.

Instead, they have a layer of thick fat called blubber to keep them warm in icy cold water. Their limbs have been modified into paddlelike extensions called flippers that help them to swim. However, like other mammals, all marine mammals breathe using their lungs. They also give birth to live young and look after their babies. Some well-known marine mammals are whales, seals, sea lions, and walruses. Whales are among the largest animals in the world. They spend their entire life in the water. They look like fish, but are very different from them in every other way.

▲ **Whales with teeth**
Toothed whales include dolphins, killer whales, sperm whales, beluga whales, and porpoises.

Whales do not have gills like fish. Instead, they breathe through nostrils, called blowholes, located on top of their head. The blowholes are kept closed underwater. Whales come up to the surface at regular intervals and open their blowholes to breathe. After taking in a few gulps of air, they dive into the water again. Like fish, whales have tail fins, but they are horizontal and are called flukes. Whales move their flukes up and down to propel themselves through the water.

Classification of whales

Whales are divided into toothed and baleen whales. Toothed whales have small, sharp teeth in their jaws. Baleen whales are toothless. Instead, they have sievelike structures, called baleen, that hang from their upper jaws. These whales swim with their mouths open, taking in water rich in krill, plankton, and other tiny marine creatures. The prey gets trapped in the comblike edges of the baleen plates and the whale licks the food off them. Baleen whales, also known as great whales, include grey whales, humpback whales, right whales, and blue whales.

◄ **Pause for breath**
Sometimes when a whale comes up to the surface of the ocean to breathe you can see a fountain shoot up from the blowhole at the top of its head. This fountain is called the blow, or spout. Contrary to popular belief, the blow is not actually a fountain of water. It is in fact stale air, which condenses and vaporizes the moment it is released into the atmosphere. The blow of some whales can shoot up to heights of 33 feet (10 meters).

▲ **A cold existence**
Leopard seals live in the waters around Antarctica.

Seals and walruses

Seals and walruses fall into one group called pinnipeds, meaning fin-footed. All species in this group have limbs that look like fins. Seals are classified into true seals and eared seals. True seals do not have external ear flaps, while eared seals do. There are 19 species of true seals, making this group the largest among pinnipeds. Eared seals include sea lions and fur seals. Seals have powerful flippers and a strong torpedo-shaped body that make them great swimmers. However, true seals are very clumsy on land, sliding on the ice with great difficulty. The rear flippers of eared seals are longer and more mobile than those of true seals and better adapted for moving on land. Their front flippers are also larger and more powerful. Eared seals use their front flippers to row through the water. Seals range in size from 3 feet (1 meter) to over 13 feet (4 meters). Galapagos fur seals and ringed seals are the smallest, while the male southern elephant seal is the largest in the world.

Seals spend most of their lives in water, but they come ashore to breed and look after their young. They mainly eat fish, squid, crab, and shellfish. However, some species, like leopard seals, also hunt other seals and penguins.

Having a whale of a time!

Whales do more than just swim and dive. They are known to leap out of the water and indulge in playful behavior. Sometimes they pop their head above the surface and float motionless. This behavior is known as "logging." Some whales, such as humpback whales and orcas, leap right out of the water, which is known as "breaching." Whales also stick their tails out and splash them around. This is called "lob-tailing." Some species, such as dolphins and orcas, can be seen popping their heads out of the water. This behavior, known as "spyhopping," is believed to give the whale a good view above the surface.

Walruses are much bigger than seals. They inhabit the Arctic regions, at the edge of the polar ice sheet. Like all marine mammals, walruses have a layer of blubber that protects them from the cold.

Sea cows

Manatees and dugongs are together called sea cows. They are large, thick-bodied mammals, which live completely in the water. They get their name from the fact that they graze on seagrass and other aquatic plants found on the seabed. Manatees have a long, rounded body that tapers toward the tail. They have a short, square snout, and are grey in color. Dugongs are very much like manatees, except smaller. Other differences between the two include the forelimbs, which in manatees are set close to the head. Dugongs have forked and pointed tails, while those of manatees are rounded at the end and paddlelike.

◄ **Handy tusks**
The most unique feature of the walrus is its tusks, which are actually a pair of elongated upper canine teeth. Walruses use these tusks not only to defend themselves, but also as hooks to climb out of the water onto the ice. Male walruses have bigger tusks, which they use during courtship fights.

▲ **Slow swimmers**
Both the manatee (pictured) and the dugong are slow swimmers and use their forelimbs and tails to move in the water. Neither of these animals have hind limbs.

Try these too:

Mammals (p 8–9),
Primates (p 10–11),
Birds (p 54–59),
Fish (p 60–63),
Reptiles (p 20–21),
Amphibians (p 22–23)

Birds

Birds, like mammals, are warm-blooded vertebrates (animals with backbones). Unlike most mammals, birds have only two legs. Their front limbs have been modified into wings that help them fly. Birds do not give birth to their young as mammals do. Instead, they lay eggs. They have strong beaks and bodies that are covered with feathers.

Key facts:

- Some birds have what is known as powder down. These are special feathers that produce a kind of powder that acts as a waterproofing agent and conditioner.

- Cuckoos are lazy birds. They do not make nests. Instead, most cuckoos lay eggs in the nests of other birds. The female cuckoo usually searches for a host bird, whose eggs are similar to hers in appearance. Once the eggs hatch, the young cuckoo sometimes destroys the other eggs in the nest to avoid being detected.

- The arctic tern travels the longest distance during migration. It covers about 18,640 miles (30,000 kilometers), traveling between the Arctic and Antarctic regions every year.

- Some birds, such as the hummingbird, have to flap their wings rapidly to help them hover. They extend their wings and flap them up and down several times as they hover near a flower, drinking the nectar. Some species of hummingbird can beat their wings as many as 52 times in one second.

Feathers are one of the most distinguishing features of birds. They form a protective cover over the bird's body. Feathers keep birds warm and keep water off their bodies. They are often brightly colored and so add to the beauty of birds. There are two types of feathers—vaned and down feathers. Vaned feathers are the ones that we see. They cover the exterior of the body. Down feathers provide the birds with insulation and are found under the vaned feathers. A vaned feather consists of a main shaft, called a rachis. A series of branches, or barbs, are attached to the rachis. The barbs branch further into barbules, which have tiny hooks called barbicels that hold the feathers together. Down feathers are soft and fluffy because they do not have barbicels. The rachis forms a hollow tubular calamus, or quill, at the base, which is attached to a follicle in the skin. The flight feathers of the wings and tail are in fact modified vaned feathers.

Built to fly

Wings are the most important feature for flight. The size and shape of the wings determine how fast and high a bird can fly. Wings can be different shapes. Elliptical wings are short and rounded and do not help birds fly very high or for very long. They help the bird to move about in confined spaces.

▶ Migration

Most birds migrate to breed or to search for food. The change of seasons often leads to a decrease in food supply. This causes birds of one particular region to move to a place where food is abundant. Even during the breeding season, migration is related to food supply since plenty of food is required to feed the growing chicks.

▼ Tearing beaks

Birds like eagles have curved beaks with hooks at the end that help to tear the flesh of their prey.

Beak

Flexible neck

Talons

Humerus

Tail

High-speed wings are short and pointed, allowing the bird to fly very fast. Most birds that soar, glide, and hover have long wings and do not have to take a run up before taking off. However, some soaring birds with shorter wings, such as eagles, vultures, and pelicans, have slots at the end that help them to take off without taxiing. As well as wings, birds have other adaptations that improve flying. The bird's skeleton is hollow and light. They have strong lungs and a very efficient respiratory system that provides them with enough energy while flying.

◀ **Young and vulnerable**
The newly hatched chicks of some species are covered with feathers and are capable of feeding on their own. However, the young ones of most birds are born blind and without feathers. These chicks are weak and need to be kept warm as well as fed by their parents. With some species, the parents swallow the food and regurgitate it at the nest to feed their young. This way the parent can carry more food and, since it is half-digested, the young birds find it easier to swallow than whole pieces.

Beaks

All birds have beaks, also known as bills. The beak is a bony structure composed of an upper jaw called a maxilla and a lower jaw called a mandible. A bird's beak varies according to the kind of food it eats. Meat-eating birds have cutting beaks that help them to tear the flesh of their prey. Hummingbirds have long, narrow beaks that help them to suck nectar from flowers. Apart from eating, birds use their beaks for many other purposes. Some, like the woodpecker, use their beaks to drum on trees to attract a mate or make hollows in trees for use as nests. Birds carry twigs for their nests and food for their young in their beaks. They also use their beaks to defend themselves.

Home sweet home

Almost all birds build nests. Some of them build nests with twigs and leaves, while others make simple holes in the ground to hide in. Certain other species use the old nests of other birds to lay their eggs in. Nests come in various shapes and sizes. They can range from simple, cup-shaped nests to elaborate dome-topped hanging nests like those of the tailorbird. A particular species of cave swiftlet makes a nest from its own saliva. This nest is the main ingredient of bird's nest soup, a delicacy in China.

Hard-working stomach!

Birds do not have teeth, so they have to swallow their food whole. How do birds break up their food? Birds have a very strong, muscular stomach called a gizzard, the muscles of which rotate the food around inside and crush it. Sometimes the bird swallows small stones or gravel to make the gizzard's work easier. These stones are called gizzard stones and break up hard food such as seeds as they are rotated inside the gizzard.

Loving father!

Most birds mate with one partner at a time, with some mating for life. After mating, the female lays her eggs in a nest usually built by her. With most species, the mother incubates the eggs, but for some birds the work is split equally between both partners. With some species, the male carries out the incubating all by himself. When not brooding, male birds stay by their nests to protect the female and the eggs and bring back food for the mother. Once the eggs have hatched, both partners take turns feeding and protecting the chicks. Male birds take more of an interest in raising their young ones than the males of most other animal groups.

▼ **Watch me!**
During the breeding season, most birds observe specific mating rituals. Some birds spread their wings and dance, while others, such as the eagle, perform complicated aerobatics while flying. Sometimes, birds undergo a change in their physical appearance during mating. For example, the male frigate bird has a red-colored inflatable pouch on its neck. The bird inflates this pouch during mating and shakes it to catch the female's attention.

Try these too:

Mammals (p 8–15),
Fish (p 18–19),
Reptiles (p 20–21),
Amphibians (p 22–23),
Insects (p 24–25)

Fish

Fish are cold-blooded vertebrates (organisms with a backbone) that live in water. They breathe with their gills. Most of them have fins for swimming, scales, and streamlined bodies. They come in a variety of sizes, shapes, and colors. Fish can be divided into jawless and jawed fish. The jawless are one of the earliest types of fish and have been around for millions of years.

Key facts:

• Like birds, fish also migrate to breed and to search for food. The salmon, which actually lives in the sea, migrates to freshwater during the breeding season. Interestingly, it is capable of traveling hundreds of miles to return to the same stream where it was born.

• The whale shark is the largest fish in the world. It grows to about 46 feet (14 meters) in length. The smallest known fish is the stout infant fish, which grows to a length of only 0.3 inches (7 millimeters).

• Fish do not usually make very good parents, but male seahorses are an exception. These creatures are great fathers. The female seahorse lays eggs in a pouch on the male's body. The males carry these eggs until they hatch.

• Some species of fish, such as minnows, can recognize the smell of chemicals that may be present on the skin of other members of the same species. When attacked, minnows release this chemical into the water to warn other minnows.

Some of the better-known species of jawless fish that survive today are hagfish and lampreys. Jawed fish are further divided into bony and cartilaginous fish. Bony fish have skeletons made of rigid bone, while the skeletons of cartilaginous fish are made of a flexible material called cartilage. Cartilaginous fish include all sharks, rays, and chimeras. There are two groups of bony fish—lobe-finned and ray-finned. Lobe-finned fish include lungfish and the prehistoric coelacanth. Other fish, like herring, tuna, and salmon, are ray-finned.

Life under water

Fish have special adaptations that are important for their life under water. Most fish have a streamlined body that is pointed at the front and tapers toward the end. They also have strong, moveable tail fins that propel them through the water. Dorsal, anal, pelvic, and pectoral fins provide the balance and thrust required to swim. Fins are in fact thin membranes that are stretched over a series of fanlike spines or rays. All bony fish have an air-filled organ called the swim bladder. This organ helps the fish to stay afloat without moving. This allows a fish to save energy, since it does not have to swim to stay in one place.

Since they spend all their lives in water, fish also have special "lungs" that help them to breathe. The respiratory organs of a fish are called gills. When water enters the mouth of a fish, it passes over the gills. The oxygen dissolved in the water is extracted and passed through the gills into the blood, while carbon dioxide exhaled by the fish is dissolved in the water. Some fish, such as lungfish, do not have gills. They breathe using lungs.

◄ **Home under water**
Fish can be found in both freshwater and saltwater environments. Freshwater rivers and lakes contain about 40 percent of the world's fish species, while the rest live in oceans. Most marine fish live either on the sea floor or in and around reefs. Very few inhabit the deepest waters.

Gills

Scales

▼ Scales to the rescue
The body of a fish is covered with scales that protect it from predators and injuries. Some fish have spines that keep their enemies away.

Try these too:

Mammals (p 8–15),
Birds (p 16–17),
Reptiles (p 20–21),
Amphibians (p 22–23),
Insects (p 24–25)

Reproduction

All fish lay eggs. However, the number of eggs, the type of birth, and the method of egg fertilization vary from species to species. Male sharks insert a sexual organ into the female to pass their sperm into her. The eggs are fertilized inside the female's body. Some sharks lay the fertilized eggs among rocks and seaweed on the ocean floor. These eggs hatch within a few days or weeks. In certain shark species, the eggs hatch inside the mother's body and she gives birth to live young. Most fish release their eggs and sperm into the water. The sperm fertilize the eggs in the water. This type of reproduction is called spawning.

◄ Spawning young
Adult salmon swim hundreds of miles back to the stream they were born in, fighting against strong currents, only to breed and then die.

A matter of sense

Like all the other animals, fish can see, smell, hear, taste, and feel. In addition to this, most fish have a sixth sense organ. This sixth sense is called a lateral line, which is a sensitive canal that runs through the length of the body of the fish from its gills to its tail fin. Tiny hairlike structures, or cilia, found on the lateral line (see right) can detect even the slightest movement in water. These then send a message to the brain, helping the fish to avoid collisions with other creatures or objects under water and to detect prey.

Cilia

Hair cell

Reptiles

Reptiles are vertebrates that share many characteristics with other animal groups. Like birds, reptiles lay eggs that have a protective outer shell, but they are cold-blooded like fish, meaning that they cannot produce their own body heat. Like mammals, reptiles breathe with their lungs and most of them have teeth. However, the similarities end there.

▸ **Getting tanned?**
All reptiles bask in the sun during the day. They often lie on a rock or log.

Key facts:

• Leatherback turtles are the largest turtles in the world. They can grow up to 10 feet (3 meters) in length and weigh over 2,000 pounds (900 kilograms). The 4 inch- (11 centimeter-) long American bog turtle is one of the smallest turtles.

• The Gila monster and the Mexican bearded lizard are the only species of lizard that are poisonous, but neither are harmful to humans since the poison is introduced slowly by chewing.

• When attacked, the Australian frilled lizard flares up the frill around its neck to display bright orange and red scales. It also opens its mouth wide to show a bright pink or yellow lining inside to scare the enemy away.

▸ **Turtle alert!**
There are seven species of sea turtles in the world, all of which are listed as endangered. Over the years, sea turtles have been hunted for their eggs, meat, and shell. The green sea turtle was extensively hunted for the cartilage, called calipee, found in its bottom shell. Calipee was used to make turtle soup.

Most reptiles do not look after their eggs or take care of their young. They also have a rough skin that is not covered with scales or feathers. Reptiles can be found almost everywhere, except the polar regions since they cannot survive there due to their cold-blooded nature. There are more than 7,000 species of reptiles, belonging to four main groups—turtles and tortoises, snakes and lizards, crocodiles and alligators, and tuataras.

Reptilian life

All reptiles have a well-developed brain and most have two lungs. All reptiles, except crocodilians, have a three-chambered heart. Crocodiles and their relatives have four-chambered hearts like mammals. The tough skin of reptiles keeps their internal organs from becoming dry and also protects the reptile from injuries.

All reptiles shed their skin periodically as they grow. Most reptiles are meat eaters and feed on a variety of prey, including insects, birds, rodents, fish, amphibians, and even other reptiles. Most reptiles wait for their prey to come close, then ambush it. Some kill their prey by suffocating it, while others bite or inject poison into their victims.

▲ **The scent of life!**
The forked tongue of a snake picks up chemical traces, which are then carried into the Jacobson's organ to be identified. This is why snakes keep flicking their tongues in and out.

Reptilian senses

All reptiles taste and smell with the help of the Jacobson's organ, found in the roof of the mouth. It is a small cavity lined with sense detectors that can recognize chemical changes in the mouth. This organ not only aids in locating prey and finding a mate, but also helps the reptile get a general bearing of its surroundings. Some reptiles rely on their eyesight to find prey. The eyes of reptiles that actively hunt are located at the front of their head to provide them with a sense of depth.

Tuatara

There are only two species of tuatara in the world today. They are the only survivors of a group of reptiles that first emerged about 225 million years ago—even before the dinosaurs came into being, which is why they are sometimes called living fossils. Tuataras are found only on a few islands off the New Zealand coast. These reptiles grow very slowly and are thought to live for as long as a hundred years.

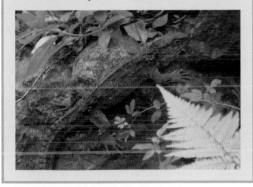

Turtles and tortoises

There are more than 250 species of turtle and tortoise. The term *turtle* is mainly used to describe the species that live in water, while tortoises live entirely on land. Tortoises and sea turtles can grow to be quite large, while freshwater turtles are often small. All of them have a protective shell made of flat bones. This shell is joined with parts of the spinal column and ribs. The upper shell is called the carapace, and the lower one is called the plastron. The two pieces are connected by a "bridge." The shell of a turtle is flatter and lighter than that of a tortoise. Tortoises usually have strong and heavy shells. Sea turtles have large flipperlike forelimbs that help them to swim underwater. Turtles are known to live very long. Some species can live longer than 150 years. Although turtles spend a lot of time underwater, they have to come up to the surface frequently to breathe. They also lay their eggs on dry land. When the eggs hatch, the young ones immediately begin their long journey from land to water.

▶ **Catch me if you can**

When in danger, the first instinct of a reptile is to hide or escape. If cornered, reptiles resort to a variety of defense tactics. Some appear larger than they really are to frighten their attacker, while others make loud noises and release foul-smelling chemicals. Most snakes, lizards, and turtles deliver a painful, sometimes poisonous, bite. Lizards, like chameleons, change their colors to escape their enemies.

Lizards and snakes

The order Squamata consists of lizards, snakes, and worm lizards. There are more than 4,300 species of lizard, making them the most diverse family among the reptiles. Most lizards have long, slender bodies and narrow, pointed tails. Almost all of them have four legs with clawed toes. However, some species have reduced limbs or no limbs at all. Most lizards feed on insects. Larger species feed on smaller reptiles and mammals, while some lizards eat plants. The other families related to lizards are snakes and worm lizards. Most species belonging to these families lack legs, but the similarity between the two ends there. Worm lizards spend most of their lives underground. They have short tails and blunt snouts that help them to dig. Some worm lizards have large front legs. Snakes are believed to have evolved from burrowing lizards. But unlike most lizards, snakes do not have external ears and moveable eyelids. Instead, their eyes are protected by transparent scales.

Crocodilians

Crocodiles, alligators, caimans, and gavials are together called crocodilians. These giant lizardlike reptiles spend most of their time in water. All families in this group have powerful, flat tails that help to propel them through the water. Their eyes and nostrils are located on top of their head. This allows these reptiles to lie submerged but still be able to breathe and keep an eye on their surroundings. It also helps them to sneak up on unsuspecting prey.

Try these too:

Mammals (p 8–15),
Birds (p 16–17),
Fish (p 18–19),
Amphibians (p 22–23),
Insects (p 24–25),
Plant Life (p 26–27)

Amphibians

Amphibians are cold-blooded vertebrates that combine the features of both fish and reptiles. There are about 6,000 species of amphibian in the world. Frogs, toads, salamanders, newts, and a small group of limbless, tropical creatures called caecilians, are all amphibians.

Adult frog

Key facts:

• Females of most amphibian species lay eggs directly in water, while some frogs, salamanders, and almost all caecilians prefer to lay eggs on land in moist places like burrows or logs. The eggs are usually suspended in a jellylike substance and are not protected by a hard shell-like cover.

• Salamanders can regenerate injured or lost body parts such as a leg or a tail.

• Some adult species of newt are able to survive in water even though they lose their gills and grow lungs.

• Adult frogs can breathe through their lungs, but they prefer to absorb oxygen through the thin lining of their mouths. In fact, in moist conditions, frogs can absorb oxygen directly through their skin.

The name amphibian means "double life," describing the ability of these creatures to survive both on land and in water. Amphibians are born in water, as they lay their eggs in water or in a moist place close to water. The larvae that hatch from the eggs are limbless. They have gills through which they breathe and they use their fishlike tails to swim. As they grow, they develop limbs and lungs that help them to survive on land. Amphibians do not have dry, scaly skin like reptiles. They have smooth, moist skin that needs to be in regular contact with water. The bodies of amphibians vary greatly, depending on the type of species and its environment. Frogs and toads have short squat bodies, with long hind legs and no tail. Salamanders and newts have longer bodies, long tails, and short legs.

Frogs and toads

Frogs have muscular, well-developed hind limbs and webbed feet, which are helpful for jumping. Most of them have smooth green or brown skins, while some rare species are brilliantly colored. Toads are distinguished from frogs by their thick skin and heavy bodies. Some varieties also have warts all over and enlarged salivary glands behind their eyes. Frogs and toads have huge, bulging eyes that are covered by transparent membranes that keep them constantly moist. Both species have voice boxes and are capable of making a variety of sounds. Frogs and toads have eardrums on each side of their heads, rather than ears. They have long forked tongues, which they whip out to catch small insects. Some of the larger varieties are known to even eat small snakes and mammals. Some rare varieties of frogs and toads can secrete poison from their skin and salivary glands.

◀ **Truly aquatic**
Some species of salamander spend their entire life in water.

▾ Aquatic metamorphosis
The eggs of a frog hatch into oval-shaped larvae called tadpoles, which live in the water as they slowly change into an adult.

Young frog (metamorph)

Tadpole with legs

Eggs

Embryo

Tadpole

Try these too:

Mammals (p 8–15),
Birds (p 16–17),
Fish (p 18–19),
Reptiles (p 20–21),
Insects (p 24–25),
Plant Life (p 26–27)

Salamanders and newts

Salamanders are smooth-skinned, lizardlike creatures that are mostly nocturnal. Most grow to only about 6 inches (15 centimeters) in length, but some, like the giant Japanese salamander, can grow up to 5 feet (1.5 meters). Newts are a type of salamander and also begin life in water, adapting to live on land as they grow up. Salamanders and newts mainly stay close to water, though some varieties live in trees, in burrows, or in caves. They feed on small insects, worms, and snails. Like frogs and toads, some species of salamander secrete poisonous or irritating substances.

▾ False salamanders
Sirens form a subgroup of salamanders, native to southern USA and northern Mexico. They have lizardlike bodies and moist skins but, unlike salamanders, sirens only have two short forelegs and no hind legs.

Caecilians

Caecilians are a small group of amphibians that resemble eels or earthworms. Most caecilians normally grow to a length of around 15 inches (38 centimeters), but rare species can grow up to 4.5 feet (1.37 meters). These wormlike creatures have no limbs and no tail. Caecilians normally live in burrows throughout their lives, which could be the reason why their eyes are shielded with a skin covering, and in some species covered with bone, making them blind. Like all other amphibians, caecilians are carnivores, but unlike the others, some species of caecilians can bear live young.

Insects

Insects are the most common life forms on the planet. There are 800,000 known insect species and millions more not fully known to science. This is more than all the mammals, birds, reptiles, amphibians, and fish put together. Insects can be found everywhere—in forests, on ponds, and in our own backyards. The only places you will not find these creepy crawlies are in the ocean and the polar regions.

Antenna

Compound eye

Wing

Key facts:

• The hard but light exoskeleton of an insect is largely made of a substance called chitin. It is made up of several layers and protects the insect from enemy attacks and changes in the environment.

• Insects feed on other insects, small animals, plants, and dead vegetable or animal matter. Some insects, like lice or fleas, are parasites, living off other animals.

• Fossils show that insects haven't changed very much since their first ancestors lived on Earth 350 million years ago, in the early Bashkirian Age. Their small sizes, ability to reproduce in large numbers, and ability to hide easily or fly away from danger are probably the reasons why they have been able to survive for so long.

• Some insects protect themselves using the method of camouflage, as in the case of the praying mantis or the stick insect. Others, such as wasps, bees, and hornets, have venomous stings that they use to defend themselves.

All insects have six legs, a pair of antennae, and a pair of compound eyes. Some insects also have wings. The body of an insect is divided into three parts—the head, the thorax, and the abdomen. The soft body of an insect is covered by a thick, protective outer layer called the exoskeleton.

Special characteristics

Insects are the only invertebrates (animals without a backbone) that can fly. Insects such as flies, mosquitoes, bees, cockroaches, and grasshoppers have wings attached to the thorax. When flying, these wings are well supported by muscles inside the thorax. The thorax also supports the legs. Insects have legs that are suited for swimming, jumping, digging, or holding, depending on the species. Their mouthparts are also varied so that they can pierce and suck (mosquitoes), bite and chew (caterpillars and beetles), or sponge (flies). The eyes of an insect are situated on top, or on each side, of their heads. Insect eyes are made up of several hundred tiny lenses. Unlike humans or other animals, insects cannot move their eyes and they are in fact quite nearsighted. This means that they cannot see very well or very far. It is the feelers, or antennae, placed above the eyes, that help insects to search for food and to warn them of danger.

▲ The truth about wings
Wings are important in identifying the different species of insects. Some, like flies and mosquitoes, have one pair of membranous wings. Butterflies and moths have wings covered with powdery scales, while the hard outer wings of beetles provide protection to their back wings.

Abdomen

Thorax

Head

▲ An eye for movement
The compound eyes of an insect might not be able to see objects that are far, but they are good at detecting fast movements. The eyes also help the insect to fly at high speeds without bumping into any object and chase fast-moving prey.

Social stomach
Crop
Hind gut
Anal gland reservoir
Rectum
Digestive tract
Brain
Large intestine
Nerve cord
Eye

Try these too:

Mammals (p 8–15),
Birds (p 16–17),
Fish (p 18–19),
Reptiles (p 20–21),
Amphibians (p 22–23),
Plant Life (p 26–27)

◀ **Insight into insects**
The digestive system of an insect consists of a tube running from the mouth to the anus. This tube is specially designed to control the amount of water in the insect's body.

The inside story

Insects have several tiny openings, called spiracles, along the sides of their bodies. Oxygen enters the insect's body through these spiracles and is circulated by thin air tubes called tracheae. The larvae of some species breathe through gills. Insects have an "open" circulatory system. Like in humans and other animals, the insect's heart pumps blood. However, the blood is not carried through the body by blood vessels. Instead, it flows freely around the internal organs and back to the heart. Insects also have a well-developed nervous system, with a brain and sense organs. Insects reproduce through eggs, which are sometimes hatched in the mother's body. In some species, females reproduce without the help of males, whereas in others, unfertilized eggs produce males and fertilized eggs produce females.

Scourge or saviors?

Most of us see insects as fearful or irritating creatures, which are responsible for spreading diseases or attacking our food supplies. Mosquitoes spread diseases like malaria and filaria, termites destroy wood, locusts destroy entire fields of food crops and weevils eat into our grain supplies. However, did you know that without insects the world would probably be filled with dead animals and plants? For example, the dung beetle is responsible for the breakdown of animal waste matter and plays an important role in cleaning up our environment. Bees and butterflies play an important role in the pollination of plants. Flowering plants bloom and food crops thrive when they are busy. Insects are also the source of useful products like honey, lac, silk, and wax.

▲ **An armor of dung**
Beetles are the largest group of insects. There are 350,000 types of beetle on Earth. The dung beetle shown here makes a ball of animal dung and drags it away to a safe place where it can lay its eggs and hide them in the ball. The dung ball protects the eggs and provides the larvae with food until they are strong enough to step out on their own.

Plant Life

Plants are one of the biggest groups of living things on Earth. Almost all plants are green in color, they cannot move and they do not have sense organs to smell, hear, see, touch, or taste, like animals or human beings. Plants appeared on Earth for the first time around 400 million years ago. Today, there are more than 300,000 types of plants on this planet.

▲ **Pretty important**
Flowers are the most attractive part of a plant and play an important role in pollination.

Key facts:

• Some plants have underground stems that send out leaves above the ground and roots below. Examples of underground stems are bulbs like onion, rhizomes like ginger, and tubers like potato.

• Plants in dry places and deserts have very few or no leaves. They are covered with spines or hairs and are thick and fleshy so that they can store a lot of water.

• Mangrove forests are found in the shallow coastal areas of some tropical countries. The trees in these forests are specially adapted to growing in salty water.

Plants are divided into four major groups, depending on the way they reproduce. They are: bryophytes (mosses and liverworts), pteridophytes (ferns, horsetails, and club mosses), gymnosperms (conifers, yews, cycads, and ginkgos) and angiosperms (flowering trees and shrubs).

Mosses and liverworts

These are small plants that grow close to the ground in moist places. They absorb water from the atmosphere to transport food around their bodies. These plants have spores in capsules at the end of long stalks. The mother plant provides food to the spores, and when the capsule, or sporophyte, dries, the spores burst out and fall onto the ground.

Ferns, club mosses, and horsetails

These first appeared in the Paleozoic era. They have stems, leaves, and roots and can transport food, water, and minerals around their bodies. This is taken care of by the vascular system, which is made up of a number of water-carrying tissues. Like the bryophytes, these plants reproduce through spores. The spores are produced and stored in sporangia, or seed sacs, on the underside of the leaves.

Conifers, cycads, and ginkgos

Conifers, cycads, and ginkgos are trees or shrubs with roots, stems, and leaves. The leaves of these trees are like needles or scales. The seeds of these plants are called "naked seeds" because they are not hidden within fruit. Instead, they are stored on cones that grow on these trees.

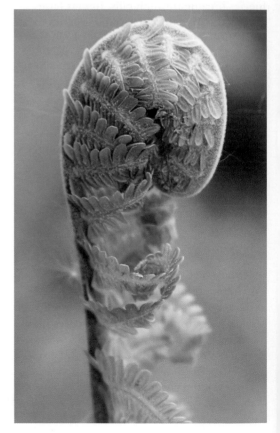

Sporangia
Frond

▶ **Bearing spores**
The developing sporangia on the underside of fern fronds are at first green in color. They slowly turn brown, black, or yellow as they mature. When ripe enough, the sporangia split open to release the spores into the air.

Flowering trees and shrubs

There are of two types of flowering trees and shrubs—monocotyledons and dicotyledons. In both these types the seeds grow in the ovary of the flower. When the flower dies, a fruit grows around the seeds. Monocotyledon seeds have single seed leaves within them. The leaves of these plants have narrow veins that are parallel to each other and do not branch out. Dicotyledons have seeds with two seed leaves and their foliage leaves have a thick main vein that branches out into several thinner veins over the leaf. Flowering and fruit-bearing plants grow in an amazing variety of sizes and forms. They can be trees (apple, mango, banyan, oak, or chestnut), woody plants (rose, hibiscus, or frangipani), green herbaceous plants (tomato, chrysanthemum, or strawberry), or vines (also called climbers) and creepers (honeysuckle, sweet pea, or pumpkin). Flowering plants can be annuals, which live only for one year and flower for three to four months (marigold, aster, phlox). They can be biennials, which live for two years and flower only in the second year (parsley, foxglove, carrot). Some plants may also be perennials, which live for many years and flower every year (water lily, begonia, banana).

Biomes

Plants can be roughly divided into three major biomes. A biome is a large area with a distinctive climate and plants and animals adapted to living in that climate. The three major biomes on Earth are the tropical forests near the equator, the temperate forests between the tropics and the polar regions, and the boreal or taiga forests just south of the Arctic.

◄ **Weak stems**
Creepers and climbers (vines) have weak stems that cannot support the rest of the plant. So these plants either creep along the ground or climb up rocks, walls, or other plants for support.

▲ **Tree basics**
Trees are tall and have branches coming out of a single stem, or trunk.

Try these too:

Mammals (p 8–15),
Birds (p 16–17),
Fish (p 18–19),
Reptiles (p 20–21),
Insects (p 24–25),
Food for Plants (p 28–29)

◄ **Not trees**
Unlike trees, shrubs have many stems and are short. They also have small branches covered with leaves.

Food for Plants

The parts of a plant consist of the root, stem, leaves, flowers, fruit, and seeds. These parts can be grouped as reproductive or vegetative parts. The root, stem, and leaves are vegetative parts. They help in manufacturing food and transporting it throughout the various parts of the plant. Flowers, fruit, and seeds are the reproductive parts. Vegetative parts can also be used to grow plants asexually—a stem cutting can grow into a new plant.

Key facts:

• Bees and butterflies carry pollen from one flower to another and deposit it on the stigma. The stigma is found on the top of the pistil, which is a long stalk that goes down to the ovary at the center of the flower. The pollen grows tubes that go downward and fertilize the seeds in the ovary.

• The banyan is an unusual tree in which the young plants grow aerial (upward growing) roots that attach themselves to another tree. Banyans normally keep spreading and have several such roots attached to them.

• Water plants, like hyacinth and lily, float on water and are not rooted in soil. Their stems, leaves, and roots have several air spaces, which make them light and help them to float. Water lily leaves have stomata on top, so that they can breathe easily.

• Flowers are the most beautiful and sweet-smelling parts of plants so that they attract insects for pollination. However, the rafflesia, which is the largest flower in the world, smells of rotten meat.

In plants with vascular systems (plants that can transport water and food on their own), the roots grow below the ground. There is a main, or primary, root with several root hairs growing out of it. Roots absorb water and minerals from the soil and send it to the stem and leaves. In some plants, like carrot and radish, the root stores the minerals, while in others, like ivy and money plants, they grow above the ground and support the plant.

The support system

The stem is the main part of the plant. It rises above the ground and supports the entire weight of the plant. The leaves, flowers, and fruit grow from it. The stem supports the plant. It also transports the water and the minerals sent up by the root to the other parts of the plant. Small shrubs and creepers have green stems while trees have woody brown stems covered by bark.

Stigma

Style

Anther

Food factories

Leaves are the food factories of a plant. They are responsible for producing food required for plant growth. Leaves come in different shapes and sizes. Some of them are simple leaves, which are attached to the stem by stalks. Others are compound leaves with several small leaflets attached to one stalk that grows out of the stem. Leaves are mostly green in color. They have a thick vein running through the middle with small veins branching out from it.

Building new generations

Buds grow at the tip of the stem or at the joints of the leaves and stem. These grow into flowers. The stalk of a flower is attached to green sepals, which hold the petals together. Inside the sepals and petals is the ovary, which contains the seeds of the plant. When the seeds are fertilized, the flower withers away and the fruit begins to grow in its place.

▶ **The root of the matter**
Food in plants is usually stored in leaves or stems, but in some plants the food is stored in the roots. In carrots, the taproot is used to store food, and in sweet potatoes the lateral roots are modified for storage.

◀ **Flower power**
The pistil, the female part of a flower, consists of stigma, style, and ovaries. The male part, called the stamen, includes the anther, or the pollen sac, and the filament that supports it.

Parasitic existence

Some plants get all of their water, minerals, and food from other plants. Such plants are known as parasites. These parasitic plants attach their roots to the roots and stem of the host plant and grow by sucking nutrients from them. As these parasitic plants do not make their own food, they do not have chlorophyll or green leaves. Some plants are partial parasites. They take water and minerals from the host plant but make their own food through photosynthesis. Mistletoe is an example of a partial parasite. Plants like rafflesia depend completely on their host.

Try these too:

Mammals (p 8–15),
Birds (p 16–17),
Fish (p 18–19),
Reptiles (p 20–21),
Insects (p 24–25),
Plant Life (p 26–27)

▼ **Self-sufficient life**
The carbon, hydrogen, and a part of the oxygen present in water and carbon dioxide is converted into glucose. The leftover oxygen is released into the atmosphere, while the surplus glucose is stored in roots, leaves, and stems for future use.

Photosynthesis

Plants make their own food by combining water from the soil with sunlight and carbon dioxide from the air. Leaves contain chlorophyll, a green substance that can absorb energy from sunlight. On the underside of leaves are several tiny openings called stomata. Leaves breathe in carbon dioxide through these openings. The carbon dioxide is combined with water and energy from sunlight to make glucose, which helps plants grow. During this process, the carbon dioxide is changed into oxygen and released into the atmosphere by the leaves.

Preying on insects

In some places, the soil might lack minerals, especially nitrogen, which is necessary for their growth. Plants that live in such places make up for the deficiency by eating insects and even small animals. Such plants are known as insectivorous plants. They are usually found in marshes and on rocks. The Venus flytrap and the pitcher plant are popular examples of insectivorous plants. Both plants have brightly colored leaves that are modified into insect traps. The pitcherlike leaves of the pitcher plant contains a liquid that dissolves the trapped insect. The top part of the leaves of a flytrap has teethlike projections. When an insect sits on this part, the leaf snaps shut, trapping the prey inside.

Sunlight   Oxygen (O_2)   Water (H_2O)

Cross-section of plant cell

Glucose (Sugar $C_6H_{12}O_6$)

Carbon dioxide (CO_2)